Moschu

PLAYTIME BOOK

Moschops®
PLAYTIME BOOK

Purnell

Contents

Moschops and Friends 5
The Tidiest of All Dinosaurs 7
Dinosaur Buff 11
Party Games to Play 12
Make a Dinosaur Mask! 14
Uncle Rex's Fight 16
Dinosaurs 20
What Am I? 24
Moschops and the Message Machine 25
Weird and Wonderful Dinosaurs 30
Living Dinosaurs 34
Moschops' Party 36
Grow Your Own Cress Name! 41
Hat's Mine! 42
It's Magic 43
The Football Game 45
Shoot For Goal! 50
Mirror Message 52
Fossils 53
Make Your Own Fossil Prints 57
Moschops' Garden 58
Make Your Own Dinosaur World 63
Moschops Goes Fishing 64
Dinosaur Path 68
Underwater 70
Grandpa Sets Some Riddles! 71
Make a Prehistoric Tree 72
Hatch Your Own Dinosaur Eggs! 73
Moschops Stays Awake 74

ISBN 0 361 05953 1

Published 1983 by Purnell Books, Paulton, Bristol
BS18 5LQ, a member of the BPCC group of companies.
Printed and bound in Great Britain
by A. Wheaton & Co. Ltd, Exeter

Long, long ago, about a hundred million years ago in fact, the world looked very different. There were no humans for a start, and there were no birds, no broad-leafed trees, not many plants . . . but there was Moschops!

Moschops is a friendly little dinosaur, about as tall as a smallish tree! He eats plants, usually **horsetails**, which are like small green ferns. He's always full of new ideas and games, but he's a little clumsy and a bit forgetful sometimes . . . Like us!

Moschops' friend is called Allosaurus, or Ally for short. He's twice as tall as Moschops and he should be very strong and fierce . . . but Ally won't eat meat like he should, and he's not very brave at all!

Grandpa Diplodocus is very big indeed! He's very old and wise . . . but he's usually sleepy.

Uncle Tyrannosaurus Rex is a very fierce dinosaur, or thinks he is. He's always giving Moschops and Ally 'fierceness lessons', but they've never been very successful!

Mr. Ichthyosaurus lives in the lake. He's very old and experienced and sometimes casts spells, when he's not busy thinking up new fish dishes! He thinks that these new dinosaurs on land will never last. . . .

Mrs. Kerry is a rather bossy, tidy dinosaur. She likes to organise everything and everyone, but it never seems to last!

Flower is the first flower in the world, and a very special one who thinks and feels. When she's happy she sings beautifully; but she doesn't talk, she just moves her petals.

THE TIDIEST DINOSAUR OF THEM ALL

It was a windy morning in the land of the dinosaurs. The whole place was covered in leaves. Everywhere!

"Time to get up!" Moschops announced, coming out of his cave, and blinking in the sunlight.

"I'll just do a small spell to tidy things up a bit," said Mr. Ichthyosaurus. "Hemiopterix, Archeoplerix, Pterodactyl," he chanted.

Flower was looking very unhappy. She was looking at a black speck in the distance.

The speck came nearer. "It's got four feet . . . and it's wearing a hat!" said Moschops.

"Oh no!" groaned Mr. Ichthyosaurus. "Better brush up your petals, Flower. It's Mrs. Kerry!"

"Good morning, everyone," said Mrs. Kerry. "Good morning, Mr. Ichthyosaurus. I see you're still in your old pond."

Flower shut up tight. "I hope this flower is in the right place," said Mrs. Kerry. "Come on, look tidy."

Mrs. Kerry got very annoyed. "Look, footsteps in my sand. How untidy! I don't know, go away on holiday for five years and you come back to chaos!"

Grandpa Diplodocus arrived. "Your spectacles are crooked. How very untidy," said Mrs. Kerry.

Mrs. Kerry made Moschops and Ally clear up the leaves and smooth the sand.

"Look," said Moschops. "I can do magic! If I go backwards I can rub my footsteps out as I go!"

Moschops did his magic trick and made a terrible mess in the sand. Ally tried it, too. "Step back, wipe. Step back. Wipe . . ."

Ally bumped straight into Uncle Tyrannosaurus Rex! They fell in a heap on the floor and sent sand flying everywhere.

Mrs. Kerry was very angry at the mess. "Oh dear," said Uncle Rex. "I've just remembered a very important appointment. Goodbye!" He hurried off.

Uncle Rex found Grandpa Diplodocus trying to hide behind a rock. "I'll hide with you, if you don't mind?" he said.

Back at the pool everything was very tidy again. Moschops and Ally were sitting gloomily in a row, their footballs at their feet.

"You see," said Mrs. Kerry. "You don't have to be untidy to enjoy yourself!"

DINOSAUR BUFF

Help Ally find Moschops and win the game of Dinosaur Buff.

PARTY GAMES TO PLAY

Dancing Monsters

This is a miming game. You and your friends must pretend to be different kinds of dinosaur. Don't forget that some dinosaurs were slow and heavy; others had spiky backs and bony heads; some flew in the skies and others swam. Some ate plants and others hunted for meat. Make the sort of noises you think that dinosaurs made. Perhaps you might like to act out the end of the dinosaurs, too.

Stick-in-the-mud!

This is a chasing and catching game to play outside. One or two people play the monsters. They have to catch the others by touching them. When someone has been caught, he shouts out: 'stuck-in-the-mud!' He has to stand still until one of his friends rescues him by crawling through his legs. If someone gets stuck four times, that person becomes a monster, and frees one of the monsters to join the other side.

Dinosaur consequences!

Each player should have a piece of paper and a pencil. Draw a funny dinosaur's head on the top of your paper, so that it takes up about a third of the space. Fold the paper over so that you can see only a bit of the neck. Exchange papers with your friends and draw a silly body on to the neck. Fold the paper and exchange it for someone else's. Draw some dinosaur legs on the bottom of the body and write a dinosaur name at the foot of the paper. Exchange papers and unroll your piece; you will see a very strange monster!

Hunt the dinosaur!

Blindfold a player and give him a stick. Everyone else should dance around him until he points his stick at someone. That dancer must catch hold of the stick. The blindfolded person then shouts out: 'I want my tea!'. The dancer must explain why he shouldn't be eaten for tea — in one sentence, and in a disguised voice. The blindfolded person has to guess who he's caught. If he guesses correctly he becomes a dancer. If he doesn't then he has to try pointing again.

Storytelling

One of the players starts to tell an exciting story, but leaves off in an interesting place. The next player has to carry on the story, and so on, until it reaches a good conclusion. You could think up a prehistoric adventure.

MAKE A DINOSAUR MASK!

1. Trace this picture on to a piece of cardboard and colour in your mask.

2. Make a hole on each side, where they are marked in the picture.

3. Find two long pieces of string and make a big knot at the end of each one, a knot big enough to stop the string slipping through the mask-holes.

4. Thread the two pieces through the two holes, so that the knot is at the front of the mask. Then put your mask on and tie the string tightly behind your head. Now scare people!

UNCLE REX'S FIGHT

There was a terrible commotion one day, down by the pond. It was a very loud and very fierce roar, followed by several others.

Ally was dozing in his cave; he heard the roar and covered up his ears. Mrs. Kerry heard it, too. She was quite frightened and hoped that the noise wasn't made by anything dangerous.

Moschops was going down to the lake to see Mr. Ichthyosaurus. But when he heard the noise he changed his mind and went home!

Grandpa Diplodocus heard it, and said to himself: "That's Uncle Rex roaring. I wonder what's got him all annoyed now?" Flower knew that only Uncle Rex could make an awful noise like that. But her petals shook all the same!

The dinosaurs gathered together to talk about what they had heard. Suddenly, Uncle Rex rushed towards them, as fast as he could. Ally took one look at his angry Uncle and hid behind Grandpa Diplodocus. He thought that it was the start of another fierceness lesson, or that Uncle Rex was going to tell him off for staying in bed late.

Uncle Rex was looking very fierce indeed, but he didn't look at Ally. Instead, he roared and jumped around a bit. When he had finished gnashing his teeth and waving his tail about, he said: "Enemy! Down by the lake! I reckon it's got Mr. Ichthyosaurus, poor chap. He wouldn't have stood a chance against anyone as horrible as that creature I saw just now. Awful, it was! Sharp teeth and mean eyes!"

"Oh," shrieked Mrs. Kerry. "Was the creature huge and fierce? Shall we prepare ourselves?" She hid behind Grandpa, too.

"You'd better go and fight him, Rex," she said, nervously. "We'll stay here and back you up!"

"Steady on," said Grandpa Diplodocus. "Man the barricades! We must protect our family home! Moschops, Ally, collect as many sticks as you can. I'll find some stones to build a wall."

"There's no time for that," cried Uncle Rex. "Fight! That's what we've got to do! Prepare yourselves, it could be a fight to the finish!"

Ally and Moschops clung timidly to each other. But they were determined to be as brave as possible. Ally felt quite grateful to Uncle Rex for giving him fierceness lessons.

"Uncle Rex," began Moschops, in a shaky sort of voice. "Do you think that your awful enemy has . . . well, has any friends — er, are there any more with him?"

"He's bound to have," said Uncle Rex, who was bouncing about waving his fists, as if he were in a boxing ring.

"There must be at least seven of them, skulking in the ferns, no doubt. That nasty type I saw down by the pond always has a few evil pals hanging around. Waiting for a night attack, I shouldn't wonder. They'll probably want to take all our horsetails and live in our caves. We must try to save Flower, too. She's the only one in the world and is very precious! Come on, everybody, and at 'em! We're wasting time!"

Timidly, Grandpa and the others followed Uncle Rex back towards the lake.

"Poor Mr. Ichthyosaurus," whis-

pered Ally to Moschops, as they crept along. "Perhaps the monster has eaten him. Or perhaps he's been taken prisoner and we'll have to rescue him from a big gang of bad-tempered dinosaurs!"

"Oh, don't," said Moschops, shakily. 'I'm frightened enough as it is! But I'm sure Mr. Ichthyosaurus is safe. He'll be hiding in the deepest part of his pond."

They reached the edge of the lake.

"There he is — and he's brought some of his friends with him!" roared Uncle Rex. "Attack!"

"Hey, steady on," said Grandpa. "That's not an enemy, Rex."

"Of course it is!" roared Uncle Rex. "See him?" Rex pointed at the water. "It's the one I saw before. A dreadful, vicious character, if ever I saw one. Just look how he's shaking his fist at me!"

"That's because you're shaking yours at him," smiled Grandpa. The others stopped feeling frightened and began to enjoy themselves. Even Mrs. Kerry started giggling.

Uncle Rex was puzzled. He stopped still for a moment, and instantly the stranger in front of him stopped as well.

"It's your reflection in the lake, can't you see?" said Grandpa Diplodocus, and began to laugh. Ally and Moschops began to laugh, too. Even Flower started to shake in amusement.

"Oh," said Uncle Rex, rather disappointed.

"Well, really," said Mrs. Kerry. "Horrible, was he? A dreadful, vicious character! Well, you said it, Uncle Rex!" She marched off.

"I was just testing you," said Uncle Rex, airily. "It's better to be prepared, you know. Of course, I knew all along. . . ."

DINOSAURS

Dinosaurs first lived over two hundred million years ago, but they disappeared sixty-four million years ago. They lived a long time before humans, who came along only three million years ago!

Dinosaurs were 'reptiles'; they laid eggs like birds do, but much, much bigger! They were cold-blooded, which meant that they could live only where it was warm. The name 'dinosaur' means 'terrible lizard'.

There were many different kinds of dinosaur, living all over the world. Some flew; others lived in water; others lived on plains or mountains. Some of them grew to enormous size; one weighed fifty tons and was forty metres high!

We know something about these ancient creatures because their remains have been found 'fossilised' in the earth. When the dinosaurs died some of them were buried in sand or mud where they fell. Their skeletons were preserved by chemicals in the earth, and these skeletons are sometimes dug up by archaeologists. Nowadays we use a refrigerator to keep meat fresh; but in Siberia woolly mammoths have been found perfectly preserved in the ice. They may have been thirty thousand years old, but their coats were still furry!

The Earth was still very young when dinosaurs lived, and it looked quite different to the way it does today. For a start, a lot of the land was joined up; it was only later that the land drifted apart. The land was quite flat, but there were a few mountains and volcanoes. The seas were much bigger than they are today; there were marshes and swamps thick with juicy green plants. It was very warm everywhere, all of the time.

In the beginning animals lived only in the seas; then the seas began to fill with creatures and it became rather crowded! So some animals developed legs, although they still lived partly in the water. Gradually these animals began to live completely on land and, very slowly, dinosaurs developed. One of the hardest things to learn about dinosaurs is their long names. Scientists name things in Latin or Greek. The names usually refer to what the creatures are like; for instance, 'hippopotamus' means 'river horse'. People from all over the world can understand Latin and Greek.

Some dinosaurs ate plants. They usually walked on all four legs so that they could reach the leaves. Another reason was that they grew too big and heavy to walk on two legs. Other dinosaurs walked on two legs and ate meat. They were very fierce and frightening, and they fought violently with other dinosaurs. If you were a small dinosaur you had to keep well out of the way! These meat-eating monsters had big hind legs to run on, and tiny front legs to hold their food. They had jaws full of sharp teeth; the only way for plant-eating dinosaurs to escape was to wade out into the water.

One of the biggest dinosaurs was 'Brontosaurus'; this means 'thunder lizard'. Because he was so heavy he probably made the ground thunder beneath him! In fact, he was as big as seven elephants! Brontosaurus had a long tail to thump his enemies with, and four stout legs to walk on. He had a long neck and a tiny head, so tiny that his mouth must have been munching plants all the time to feed his large body. If one of his enemies came along he was able to wade into deep water, and keep his head above the waves so that he could see what was going on.

Some dinosaurs developed strange-looking armour-plating to protect themselves, and some had huge horns for fighting.

It wasn't all that safe in the water, either. There were some fierce swimming reptiles who ate fish. Some sea-serpents were up to seventeen metres long, with long necks and tails and large paddles. They had small heads and lots of teeth.

In the air there were some nasty creatures, too. At first they were small, but they had long jaws full of teeth. Then they lost the teeth and grew pointed beaks. They didn't have any feathers; instead they had wings of skin which helped them to glide.

Why dinosaurs disappeared

Dinosaurs liked warmth; but very slowly the Earth got colder. There were less plants to eat, so the plant-eaters suffered, and because they did, the meat-eaters suffered too. Another possible reason for the death of the dinosaurs was that they laid their eggs on the ground and left them unprotected. The baby dinosaurs would soon be eaten by bigger ones. Some scientists say that a disease might have spread and killed off the dinosaurs. However, we will never know exactly why these huge creatures disappeared. But perhaps we should be quite thankful because it gave humans a chance to develop, and you wouldn't like to meet a twenty metre high monster, would you?

Dinosaur fakes

In early times when men found dinosaur bones they didn't know what they were. They thought they had found dragons or giants. Because so little is known about dinosaurs some scientists have made clever fakes in order to make some money. Such a man was Dr. Albert Koch. He claimed that he had found the remains of a great sea-serpent, and he made quite a lot of money showing it. In fact, the skeleton was made up of the bones of a whale and several other animals! One German scientist, Dr. Beringer, was tricked by someone who brought him some stones, which they said that they had dug up from a nearby hill. The stones had patterns and signs on them. Later, many more stones were found on the same hill. In fact, they weren't fossils, as Dr. Beringer had thought. They had been put on the hill by the doctor's enemies, who had carved them only days before. There was a big trial in the law-courts and the culprits were punished. Dr. Beringer finally realised he was being tricked when he found a stone with his own name carved on it!

WHAT AM I?

Look at the pictures and decide what they are. Write the first letter of each answer down in order and you will find a hidden word!

1

2

3

4

5

6

1. fish 2. lizard 3. ostrich 4. whale
5. egg 6. Rex word = flower

MOSCHOPS AND THE MESSAGE MACHINE

One morning Grandpa Diplodocus was looking for Mrs. Kerry. He went down by the pond; he looked into the caves and he called out: "Mrs. Kerry! Where are you?" But Mrs. Kerry was nowhere to be seen.

Grandpa was rather annoyed that Mrs. Kerry was not around, he wanted to ask her something.

"Why couldn't she have told me she was going somewhere, before she went?" he said crossly.

Moschops came along to see what all the fuss was about.

"But where were you when she went, Grandpa?" asked Moschops. "Perhaps she couldn't find you either. Just like you can't find her now!"

This rather confused Grandpa. So Moschops smiled and went off to look for Mrs. Kerry. Just as he left who should come along but Mrs. Kerry!

"Ah, there you are!" said Grandpa. "Did Moschops give you my message?"

"Moschops? I haven't seen him," said Mrs. Kerry. "I've only just got here. Oh, here he is now."

Grandpa began to look even more confused.

"I just wanted to . . ." he began.

But Mrs. Kerry interrupted him. "Go and wash, Moschops," she said. "It's nearly time for lunch. Have you seen Ally. I want to tell him something."

"Now, what was it you wanted?" Mrs. Kerry turned to Grandpa.

"I can't remember," said Grandpa. "Bother it! I've been so busy looking for you that I've completely forgotten it. . . ."

Just then Uncle Rex stomped over to them. He looked rather angry, and he had his paws full of sticks.

"Mrs. Kerry, I've been looking for you all morning. What shall I do with all these dry sticks that I've tidied up. You asked me to do it, you know," he complained. "What a waste of a morning! Here you are — you can do what you like with them now!"

Uncle Rex dropped all the twigs; they fell all over the place!

"Humph!" he said, and marched off.

"Dear me, he does sound cross," said Mrs. Kerry. "But I'm too busy to worry about it now. I need to find Ally to tell him something."

Moschops came back, looking much cleaner.

"Ally's having a swimming lesson with Mr. Ichthyosaurus," he said.

"I saw them at the lake, while I was washing. What are all these twigs for?" he said, poking some of the sticks that Uncle Rex had dropped.

"Oh, it's just some of Uncle Rex's rubbish," said Grandpa. "Just move them out of the way, that's a good chap."

Moschops dragged some of the sticks across the ground and dumped them by a patch of fern. He began to walk back, but stopped and looked down.

"Gosh!" he cried. "One of the sticks was touching the ground as I walked, and now you can see just where I've been!"

Sure enough, there was a line drawn in the sand, all the way to the patch of ferns.

"Look, another one!" said Moschops. He had found another line, drawn by a stick in the soil. "This must be where Uncle Rex walked with the sticks. I say, Mrs. Kerry! If we walked about with sticks, leaving trails on the ground, everyone could find us when they wanted us for something!"

"But not on hard ground," said Grandpa.

"Or through thick bushes," said Mrs. Kerry.

"Oh," said Moschops, rather disappointedly. "But if we drew something like this . . ." He picked up one of the sticks and drew a wavy mark in the sand. "We could leave messages saying where we had gone!"

"How could we do that?" asked Grandpa.

"Well, this could be a lake." Moschops drew a round circle in the sand. "And this could be a mountain . . . see?" He drew a hump-shape in the soil.

Everyone gathered round admiringly. "What a good idea," said Mrs. Kerry. "Now no one has any excuse for disappearing when I have some jobs that need doing!"

Grandpa Diplodocus sighed. Sometimes, he thought, Moschops was just a little bit too clever!

Lots of strange-looking creatures lived at different times on prehistoric Earth. Here are some of them:

Struthiomimus

This dinosaur looked very much like an ostrich and its name means 'ostrich imitator'. Its head looked like a bird's and it probably walked in a jerky birdlike way. It wasn't a very friendly dinosaur because it probably stole other creature's eggs to eat.

Andrias Scheuchzen

This creature lived about eight million years ago; it was a giant lizard. The remains of one was dug up in the eighteenth century, and people thought that it was the skeleton of a strange man who had survived Noah's flood!

Dimetrodon
This creature was a fierce meat-eater with very sharp teeth. The high sail on its back helped to keep it comfortably cool or warm.

Kuehneosaurus
This was a brightly-coloured lizard, with a piece of skin stretched across it, that allowed it to float like a glider for short distances.

Fighters
Here is a picture of a fearsome battle going on between two dinosaurs. Terrible scars of fights like this have been found on dinosaur remains.

Pteranodon

Pteranodons glided through the sky, looking out for food on the ground or in the sea. Although this creature was dangerous in the air, it couldn't walk very well on the ground.

Trachodon

This name means 'rough-toothed'. The animal had two thousand teeth, in fact! It wasn't as fierce as it sounds because it only ate plants and used its teeth for grinding. The Trachodon had webbed feet and spent most of its time in the water to avoid its enemies.

Triceratops

This name means 'horn-faced'. The Triceratops was a good fighter; it had huge horns and a bony shield that protected its neck.

Brachiosaurus

Brachiosaurus was the biggest and heaviest of all dinosaurs, as high as a three-storey building! It was so heavy it could only drag itself slowly around on land, and spent most of its life in water.

LIVING DINOSAURS

Although most dinosaurs died out many millions of years ago, there are still some reptiles surviving today which are closely related to them. Tortoises and Turtles are among the oldest creatures in the world. They were protected by their bony armour, and survived when others were killed. They actually live for a long time anyway; the Giant Tortoise can live up to one hundred and fifty years! They move only about four metres a minute, so if they tried to cross a road they wouldn't live for very long! King Crabs are another example of a 'living fossil'. They are found on the East coast of North America where the sea is warm. They are rare these days but they were very common five hundred and seventy million years ago!

Crocodiles and Alligators descend from the 'Euparkeria', a little reptile found two hundred and twenty million years ago. That should give the crocodiles something to smile about!

Lizards and Snakes are the largest group of living reptiles. The lizards are the oldest; they often have legs and eyelids, which snakes don't have. There are many different kinds of lizards and snakes; some are good at camouflage, others can swim or jump.

There is one contemporary monster we don't know about. Scientists say that if there is a monster in Loch Ness it could be a descendant of the dinosaurs.

MOSCHOPS' PARTY

Mr. Ichthyosaurus popped his head out of the sparkling water one day. "Sunshine, nothing but sunshine," he said.

Moschops bounced out of his cave. "Sunshine, I love a bit of sunshine!" he said.

He skipped down to the lake. "Oh, I do like to be beside the seaside," he sang. "Oh, I do like to be beside the sea!"

"Did you say sea?" said Mr. Ichthyosaurus. "This is a lake, much more comfortable than the sea!"

"What day is it today?" said Moschops. "Are days different?" Mr. Ichthyosaurus replied.

"Flower, do you know?" said Moschops. Flower was very beautiful and red. But she couldn't speak; she only sang.

From a dark and comfortable cave came the sound of snoring. It was Allosaurus, fast asleep.

"Ally!" shouted Moschops. "Ouch, must you shout!" said Ally. "What kind of day is it?" said Moschops.

"It's a sunny day," said Ally. "A sunny day for sleeping." And with that he yawned and went back to sleep.

Moschops climbed onto Grandpa's back to speak to him. "What sort of day is it?" he said.

Grandpa slowly yawned. "A sun day," he said. "A day for doing nothing."

"A Sunday!" Moschops cried, sliding happily down Grandpa's back. "Sunday is a day for giving parties," he said.

"Mr. Ichthyosaurus, will you come to my party?" said Moschops. "But I can't get out of this lake," said Mr. Ichthyosaurus sadly.

"We'll bring the party to you!" said Moschops. "Flower can come, too, we'll invite everyone!"

Grandpa Diplodocus was very excited at the thought of a party. "We can play Dinosaur Buff!" he said.

"Oh no!" said Mr. Ichthyosaurus. "Dinosaur Buff means great dinosaurs blundering around!" Flower shut up tightly.

Grandpa was blindfolded. "I'm coming!" he shouted. He was just about to step on Flower!

Moschops took the blindfold off quickly. "Caught you!" said Grandpa Diplodocus triumphantly.

It was Ally's turn. "I'll get you!" he shouted excitedly, as he ran round in circles.

He tripped over and went headlong into Uncle Rex! "I've caught you, Moschops!" he said.

"Moschops! What do you mean by calling me that brainless vegetable-eating nincompoop!"

Uncle Rex soon began to smile. "Let's all sing," he said. "Are we ready . . . one, two, three . . ." They all sang at the tops of their voices.

Flower began to sing: "Three blind mice, three blind mice . . ."

"The noise is terrible!" said Mr. Ichthyosaurus. "I think I preferred it when they were all asleep!"

GROW YOUR OWN CRESS NAME!

You need: A piece of flannel, lint or blotting paper
Scissors
A plate
Some mustard and cress seeds.

Dampen a large piece of flannel, lint or blotting paper. Put it flat on a plate and sprinkle the cress seeds over it, in the shape of your initials. Put the plate on a window ledge, and keep it moist by pouring a little water on to the plate every day. Soon the cress will grow in the shape of your initials, and you can eat the green tops of the plants in a sandwich!

Hat's mine!

Which hat belongs to which dinosaur?

It's magic!

Mr. Ichthyosaurus is casting one of his spells and making a wish. Chant the spell and make your own wish. Then turn the page and see what Mr. Ichthyosaurus was wishing for!

"RHAMPHORHYNCHUS, PODOKESAURUS
I'M GOING TO WISH FOR SOMETHING FOR US!"

THE FOOTBALL GAME

Moschops and Grandpa Diplodocus were playing football against Ally and Uncle Rex. What's more, they were winning! At half-time the score stood at 42 goals to Moschops and Grandpa, and only three to Ally and Uncle Rex.

"It's not fair!" said Ally, when they all stopped for a rest before beginning the second half.

"The young fellow's right," agreed Uncle Rex. "Downright unsportsmanlike behaviour, if you ask me."

They both glared at Grandpa Diplodocus.

"What are you talking about?" asked Moschops in amazement. "What's wrong with the way we're playing?"

"Well, just look at him," said Uncle Rex, pointing at Grandpa. "He's so big that he doesn't even have to move about the pitch!"

"That's true," said Ally. "He can head the ball into the net at one end, and still keep his tail end in goal at the other!"

"Pardon me," interrupted Grandpa. "But I didn't know there was any rule in the game which stopped one player being larger than another."

"Huh!" said Uncle Rex, who knew that there wasn't any such rule. "Come on then — let's get it over with. Time for the second half."

The others followed him. Moschops looked at Ally and shrugged.

"Sorry, Ally, but if you've got a good player, you have to play him in the team," said Moschops, with a grin.

Mr. Ichthyosaurus came to the edge of the pool to referee. He whistled, and the game began.

It was the same pitch, the same sunny afternoon, and the same players that had played in the first half. Yet somehow the second half was quite different from the first. Uncle Rex was annoyed. And when Uncle Rex was annoyed, he was at his very best.

Wham! The ball shot over Grandpa's tail and hit the back of the cave, which they were using for a goal.

Uncle Rex picked up Ally and danced around with him excitedly. Moschops trudged sadly back to the centre spot and Grandpa asked: "What happened?"

A minute later, Ally scored with a huge kick that no one could have stopped.

Uncle Rex got another. And another. And then Ally got three more.

Moschops decided to have a team talk. He and Grandpa huddled together secretively in the middle of the pitch, while Ally and Uncle Rex showed off by practising clever tricks with the ball.

"Grandpa," said Moschops. "Either we're doing something wrong or they've found a way of playing much better. Why aren't we doing so well in the second half?"

"Well, I think it's probably because we were winning so easily just now," replied Grandpa. "I don't seem to be so excited now as I was at the beginning of the game."

"Oh, I see," said Moschops. "And Ally and Uncle Rex were losing so badly they're trying much harder. That's the trouble with being a successful team—people are out to beat you! Well, we're going to lose if we're not careful and it will look worse because we threw the match away!"

They started to play again, but Uncle Rex and Ally were so determined to level the score that they played really well and kept on scoring. Ally dribbled the ball expertly down the pitch and passed it deftly to Uncle Rex, who was waiting to head it into the goalmouth. They were so fast that Moschops couldn't keep up!

Moschops got rather worried; he got the ball and passed it to Grandpa. It rolled past his nose and over the mossy line that showed where the edge of the pitch was.

"Grandpa!" yelled Moschops. There was no reply, except for a slight snore.

Grandpa Diplodocus was asleep!

Uncle Rex and Ally jumped about with glee.

"I don't think," said Uncle Rex, smugly, "that there is any rule in this game which says that all players should be fully awake throughout."

Then he headed yet another goal!

Moschops spent the rest of the game acting as goalkeeper. From time to time Grandpa woke up, but not for long, and the final score was 68—42 to Ally and Uncle Rex.

Grandpa was still asleep at the final whistle, so the others walked home without him.

"What this game needs," said Moschops thoughtfully, "is a rule which lets you send a sleepy player home and put someone in his place."

And the others agreed, knowing very well that Grandpa might be on their side one day.

SHOOT FOR GOAL!

You can play football like Moschops and Ally, but without even going outside! You must have two players. Cut out eight small circles from cardboard or use tiddlywinks. Divide them into two teams of four, colour

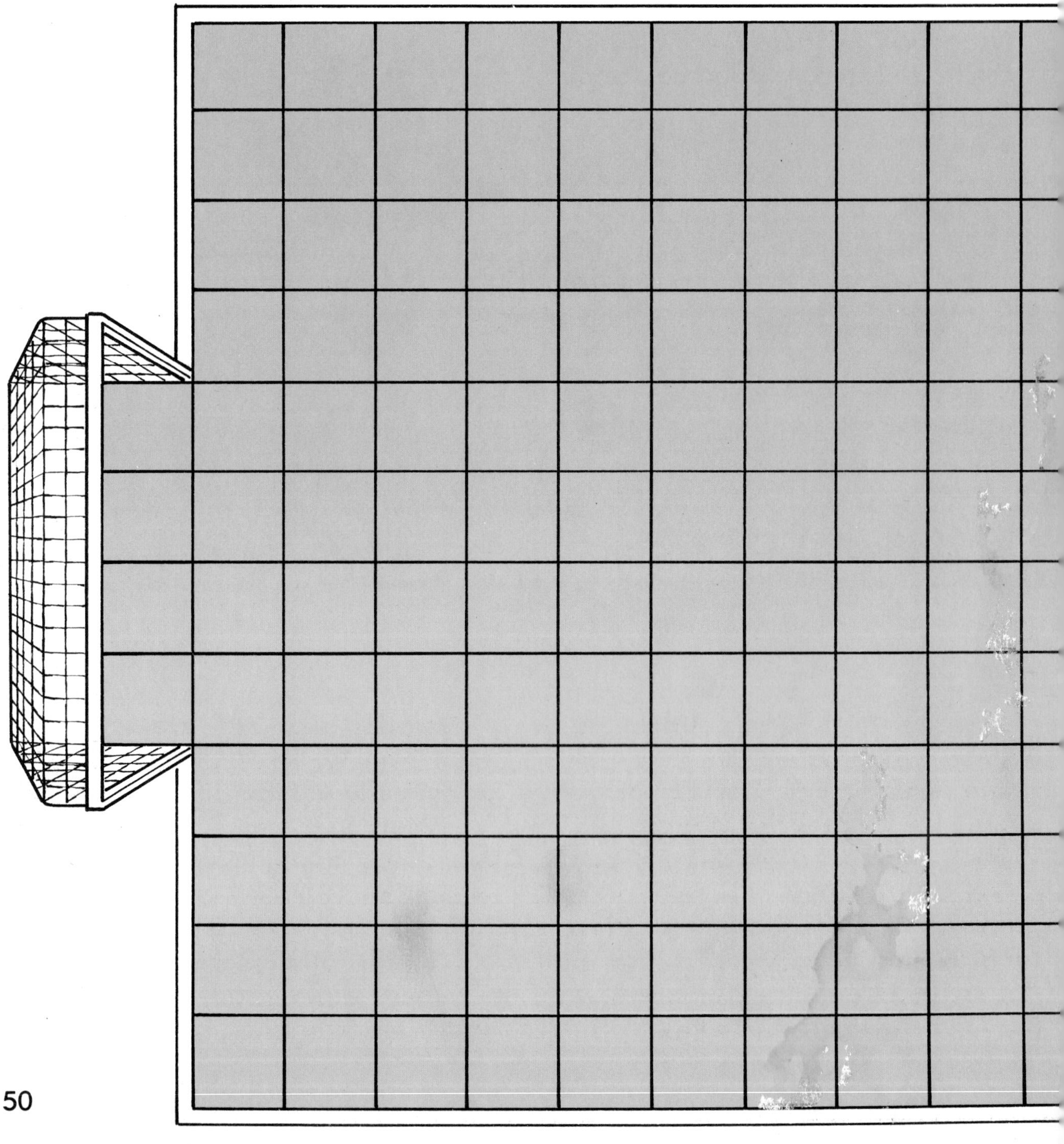

them so that you won't get the two sides mixed up. Put your four counters inside one of the goals; you must start from here. You must get all your counters into the other goal before your friend. Throw a dice to find out how many squares you can move in each turn. You cannot go on the same square as the opposing player, but you can move backwards and forwards, diagonally and sideways!

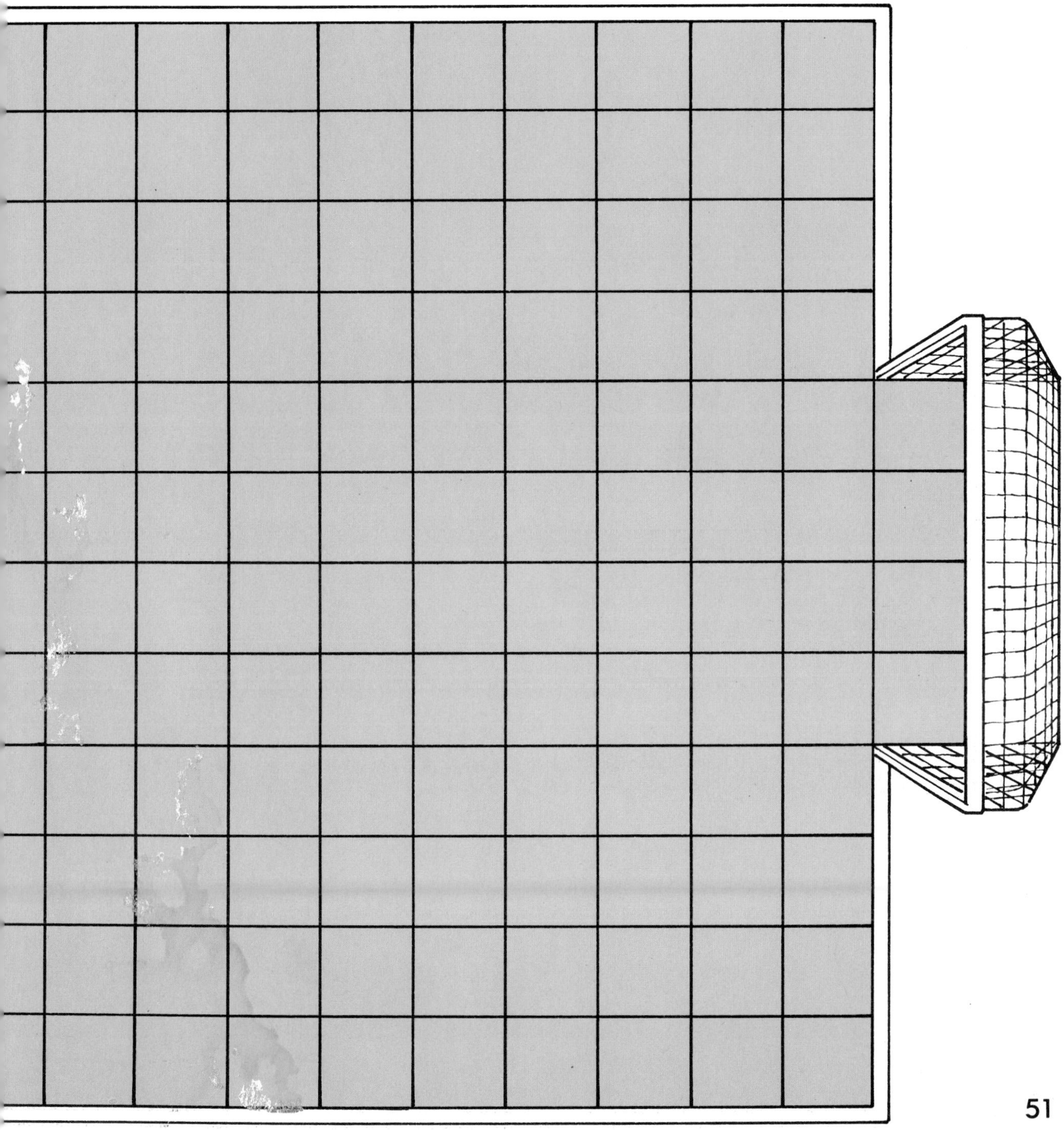

Mirror message

What is Ally dreaming of? Hold a mirror up to the words, you will see the answer in the mirror.

(Horsetail sandwiches)

FOSSILS

The word 'fossil' means 'dug up'. To become a fossil, a plant or an animal must be covered with mud or sand when it dies. Quite often animals fell to the bottom of lakes, where they were soon buried. The soft parts of an animal soon disappear, but its bones are full of pores, little holes, through which chemicals gradually seep. This makes the bones much harder, and very often they are completely replaced by rock. If this happens the bones are said to have 'petrified', or turned to stone. This often happens to trees, and sometimes whole petrified forests are found. Coal is made up of the remains of trees and plants. Where coal seams are found we know that it must once have been warm, so that lots of plants grew.

Another way that fossils are made is when a plant or an animal is pressed against a rock, so that its shape is imprinted on that rock. There are one or two other sorts of fossil. In Los Angeles, USA, there are some tar pools. Water collects on top of the tar, and in prehistoric times many animals came along to drink, and ended up getting stuck! The remains of many creatures have been found there, including the bones of a Sabre-toothed Tiger. Nowadays the pools are fenced off to stop similar accidents! One other source of fossils is amber, the resin of Pine trees. Very old amber has been found as hard pebbles, and prehistoric insects can sometimes be found stuck inside.

Some rocks are made up of fossils. During prehistoric times shells and animal skeletons fell to the bottom of the sea. They were packed down and gradually hardened to become limestone. The sea washes up shells on to beaches and sand banks. This has happened many times in the past, and the shells have gradually built up. Some of the cliffs in England are made up of shells, fossils and sand.

Where to find fossils

There aren't many fossils in hard rock, like granite. This has been formed by hot lava from inside the earth, and very rarely holds fossils. The softer sorts of rock, like clay, limestone and sandstone, are better. The best places to look for fossils are down by the beach, or in places where the earth has been dug up. Geologists have special tools for digging out fossils, but it's quite easy to spot little fossils that you can just pick up.

Some common fossils

Graptolites: Found in very fine rocks, like mudstone, shale or slate. They are the remains of sea creatures. The land where they are found was probably once under water.

Trilobites: Complete fossils are very rare, but quite often a mould of the creature is found, usually in limestone and sandstone. It looks like a woodlice with an armour-plated head.

Brachiopods: These look like flat shells. They once lived in coral seas, and sometimes they are called 'devil's toenails'!

Corals: All sorts of corals are found. You may find a strip of coral made of tiny pieces put together, looking like a little bead.

Echinoids: They are often found in chalky areas, and once looked like sea-sponges.

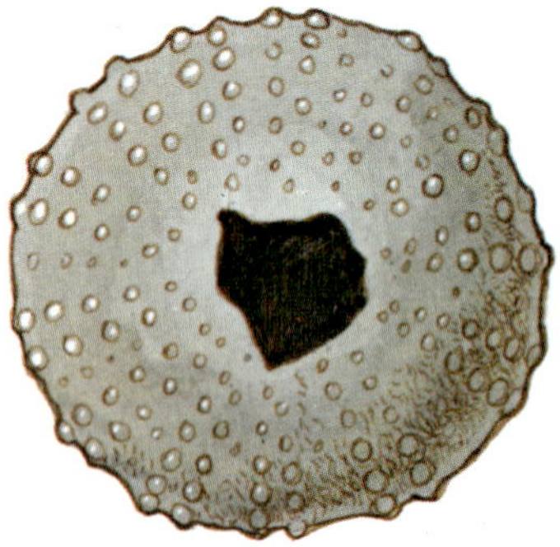

Make your own Fossil prints

1. Make a little square of plasticine or clay, about 7cm. deep. Then press something into the block, perhaps a shell with an interesting shape, or a plant (do this very gently or it will break). If you go on a trip to the beach collect all you can to make interesting fossil prints.

2. When you have pressed the object into the mould lift it out carefully and you will have a fossil print! If you are pushing quite a large object into the block it might be a good idea to make it slippery. Rub your finger on a piece of soap and then rub it all over the object. Then you should be able to get it out of the block more easily. If you use clay to make the block you will have a lasting print.

3. Making plant prints is quite easy. Dip one side of a leaf or flower in paint, and then press it down on to clean paper. Peel it off carefully and you will have a detailed picture of the leaf, just as though it was printed on a rock.

MOSCHOPS' GARDEN

It was going to be a very beautiful day in the land of the dinosaurs. The Sun rose orange and glowing over the hills, over Flower, who was closed up tightly, over Mr. Ichthyosaurus snoring gently. In fact, everyone was still fast asleep except Moschops. He was up looking for some breakfast. Moschops loved to eat horsetails, which were sort of green ferny plants; they usually grew in nice, juicy clumps by the lake. But today Moschops couldn't see any, not a single horsetail.

"Hey, Mr. Ichthyosaurus. Are you awake?" He nudged Mr. Ichthyosaurus, who had been enjoying a nice doze in the sunlight, with his tail paddling in the cool water.

"Of course I'm awake," he said, with his eyes shut.

"Seen any horsetails around here?" asked Moschops.

"I wouldn't know about those," mumbled Mr. Ichthyosaurus. "I was dreaming about fish."

That was no good to Moschops because he only ate plants, except Flower, of course.

Grandpa Diplodocus was awake, too, and very hungry. "Mmm, time for breakfast, I think," he said. "Now, where is Allosaurus. ALLY . . ." he boomed. Ally popped his head sleepily out of his cave and blinked in the light. "There you are," said Grandpa Diplodocus. "Have you seen a nice green clump of horsetails anywhere?"

"No, as a matter of fact I haven't. They're very hard to find these days." He yawned.

"Oh dear," said Grandpa. "The trouble is that there are too many big dinosaurs eating too few horsetails

you know. We may have to move on to fresh fields and pastures new," he added sadly.

Ally looked very worried indeed. "This is an emergency!" he thought. "I'd better find Moschops and work out a plan!"

He found Moschops doing a very peculiar thing; he was making holes in the sand with his tail and planting a tiny horsetail in each one. "This gardening is hard work. Twenty-one . . . twenty-two . . ." he counted.

Ally rushed up to him. "Stop playing, Moschops! We've got an emergency on our hands! Not enough food . . . have to move on . . . leave Flower and Mr. Ichthyosaurus!" he gasped.

"We can't do that!" said Moschops. "Don't worry, I've got some food here. It's not ready yet, but . . .!"

Ally rushed off to tell Grandpa that they could stay.

Meanwhile news had spread. Mr. Ichthyosaurus was leaning on his fin, a tear in his eye. "Oh dear, Flower," he said. "There's nothing for them to eat. It's all right for us, you only need rain and I only need fish." Flower was very upset. "Don't cry," sniffled Mr. Ichthyosaurus. "I'll look after you. I'll try a spell to solve everything. Typothorax, Tylosaurus, Massopondyles . . ." he chanted.

Ally came back to see the new garden and Moschops showed him what to do. "Make a hole . . . break a Horsetail . . . put it in . . . like this," he said. "Then they grow!"

Ally looked at Moschops and then he looked at the horsetails dubiously. "They aren't growing. They're the most miserable plants I've ever seen!" he said.

Moschops thought for a moment and then shouted triumphantly: "Plants! Ally . . . you're a genius! Come on!" He rushed off down to the lake, with Allosaurus behind him, looking very puzzled but quite pleased that he was a genius.

"Mr. Ichthyosaurus. Can you make your biggest splash for us?" said Moschops.

Mr. Ichthyosaurus replied gloomily: "What for? I only splash when I'm happy and I'm not happy at all."

"But if you make a splash we can all stay! Please, Mr. Ichthyosaurus!" said Moschops.

Mr. Ichthyosaurus cheered up and made the biggest splash he'd ever made. The water flew everywhere; the horsetails were soaked, and they began to spring up firmly and strongly.

"Plants need water!" cried Moschops, happily. "Come on, let's plant some more!"

Grandpa Diplodocus came along. "Oh good! Some horsetails!" he said, and started munching Moschops' garden!

"Don't, Grandpa!" cried Moschops. "This is my garden. Please don't eat it."

"Oh, your garden, is it?" said Grandpa. "What a clever dinosaur you are. Of course cleverness runs in the family, you know. Fancy, a garden! I didn't think we would see one so soon."

Mrs. Kerry arrived. "What do you think you're doing?" she said, in a stern voice.

"We're gardening," said Moschops.

"Is that what you call it. Well, you're not doing it very well. You're knocking the horsetails down as soon as you've planted them!"

And sure enough, as fast as Moschops planted a horsetail Ally dug it out to make a hole!

"Come on, a bit of tidiness, that's what's needed here!" said Mrs. Kerry. "Plant in a line . . . one, two, three . . . and you're not to eat them, Grandpa Diplodocus!" she ordered.

Everyone was very pleased because the horsetails were growing up straight and strong.

"We won't have to go away now!" smiled Moschops.

"I knew my spell would work! It always does, one way or another!" said Mr. Ichthyosaurus.

MAKE YOUR OWN PREHISTORIC WORLD

Find a deep tray, a wide biscuit tin or a box. Fill it with sand and gravel. Then make a pool, by pressing a piece of tin foil down into the sand to make a cup. Perhaps you could find an old tin foil plate and put that into the sand, so that the sand makes banks around its edges. Fill it with water and put a few stones and pieces of gravel in the bottom.

You can push bits of plant into the sand to make a garden. Use lots of different leaf shapes and sizes; some can be trees, others can be ferns. You could make 'caves' from stones, where monster dinosaurs can hide. You could even make a swamp in one part of the garden by making a hollow in the sand and filling it with some nice, messy, wet mud! Don't forget that plants grew in the swamps, too.

When you've finished your prehistoric garden you can make monsters from plasticine, or cut them out of cardboard, colour them and stand them up in the sand.

MOSCHOPS GOES FISHING

One bright day Moschops went down to see Mr. Ichthyosaurus, who was sunbathing in his pool.

"Hello," said Moschops. "You look very comfortable."

"Yes, it's a nice life, here in the water," said Mr. Ichthyosaurus. "I'm always cool, and I have plenty of fish to eat. Why, only this morning I had a very pleasant breakfast of catfish and crabs' legs."

Moschops didn't think that sounded very pleasant at all. He much preferred to eat juicy green Horsetails that didn't need catching first.

"I feel sorry for land dinosaurs," said Mr. Ichthyosaurus. "Walking round, getting all hot and bothered. Your feet must get very sore when you stand on hard ground all day. And you don't get many fish to eat, do you. You have to chew on that dull green stuff. The same thing every day, how boring!"

"I suppose you're right," said Moschops. "We do eat the same thing every day. What's it like in the water?" he asked.

Mr. Ichthyosaurus smiled and splashed about happily.

"It's hard to explain," he said.

"It feels sort of soft and squidgy, and wet, of course. Can you swim?" he asked.

Moschops couldn't swim, and he never went into the water because

he hadn't been taught.

"Don't worry, Moschops," said Mr. Ichthyosaurus. "I'll teach you to swim. Put your foot into the water and splash it about, like this."

Moschops poked his toe in the water. It felt very cold. He wiggled his foot about and made lots of little ripples appear. "It's quite fun to play with water, but I don't think that I would like to get in and swim. How do you catch fish?" he asked.

"Ah, now, that's an art, that is," said Mr. Ichthyosaurus.

"I usually surprise them by hiding behind rocks and jumping out. I'm an expert, you know. You land-animals have lost the knack. If you wait here I'll go and get a fish for you to try." He splashed confidently and dived down below the water.

Moschops waited patiently. He looked down into the pool to see if he could see Mr. Ichthyosaurus. But he could see only his own reflection, made wobbly by little waves.

Suddenly, there was a green flicker, and a fish swam past quickly. Moschops jumped and pulled his foot out of the water, pulling the fish up at the same time! It wriggled and jumped and fell on Moschops' nose!

Just at that moment Grandpa Diplodocus came along with Uncle Rex.

"What are you . . . oh!" Grandpa cried, as the fish, wriggling and squirming, landed on his nose!

"I'll get it, don't panic!" said Uncle Rex, swiping at Grandpa's nose.

"Ouch!" cried Grandpa, as Uncle Rex hit him. The fish jumped into Uncle Rex's other paw. It wriggled around, and Uncle Rex wriggled around with it, trying to catch hold of it properly.

Mrs. Kerry arrived and looked on in amazement. She couldn't believe what she saw; Uncle Rex was juggling with a fish!

"What will you get up to next!" she said.

Uncle Rex made a great effort, and threw the wriggling fish back into the water, falling over himself and landing in the pond. He made a very big splash.

"Help!" he said. "I can't swim!"

Grandpa quickly grabbed Uncle

Rex by the scruff of the neck, and pulled him out. He looked very wet and sorry for himself.

Just then Mr. Ichthyosaurus reappeared. "I couldn't find any fish,

Moschops," he said. "I thought I saw a really big one, just here, but it got away. Obviously there aren't any fish today, otherwise I would have caught one."

He looked at Uncle Rex.

"You look wet," he said. "Have you been trying to fish? Leave that sort of thing to me, Rex. You'll never catch anything!"

DINOSAUR PATH

Here is an exciting prehistoric game to play with your friends. Place a coloured cardboard counter at the beginning, one counter for each person playing. Throw one dice and move your counter the correct number of squares. You must obey the writing in the square you land on.

GET LOST in DESERT MISS 1 GO!
EARTHQUAKE GO BACK TO START
Horsetails Ahead MOVE ON 1 SPACE for LUNCH
START
FIND A WAY THROUGH BOULDERS MISS 1 TURN
Thunderstorm Take shelter Miss 1 go!
Finish

Underwater

Here is an underwater scene, full of weird and wonderful prehistoric animals. Can you find two animals that are the same?

GRANDPA SETS SOME RIDDLES!

How many fish can you get into a small, empty pool?
One; after that the pool wouldn't be empty.

Why do animals lay eggs?
Because if they let them drop they would break!

What is covered in wrinkles when it's still young?
A prune.

What kind of animal can jump higher than a tree?
All kinds. Trees don't jump!

What's the first thing you put into a garden?
Your foot.

What gets lost everytime you stand up?
Your lap.

Make a prehistoric tree

The sort of trees that grow around Moschops' cave are like Palm trees. You can make one from a piece of paper, Sellotape and scissors. There are four diagrams to help you.

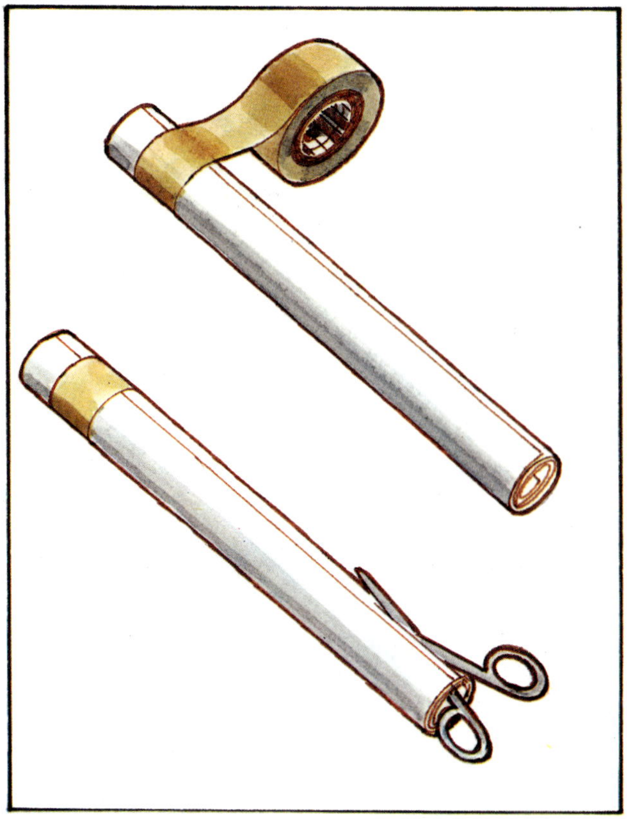

1. Roll the paper into a tight tube and sellotape one end firmly. Make sure it's secure or your tree will soon collapse!

2. Cut down the un-sellotaped end of the tube to make strips which stop about 10cm. from the sellotaped end.

3. Keep doing this until you have cut strips all the way round the tube.

4. Bend the strips down — then pull them upwards gently from the centre, but don't pull too hard! Your tree will grow before your eyes.

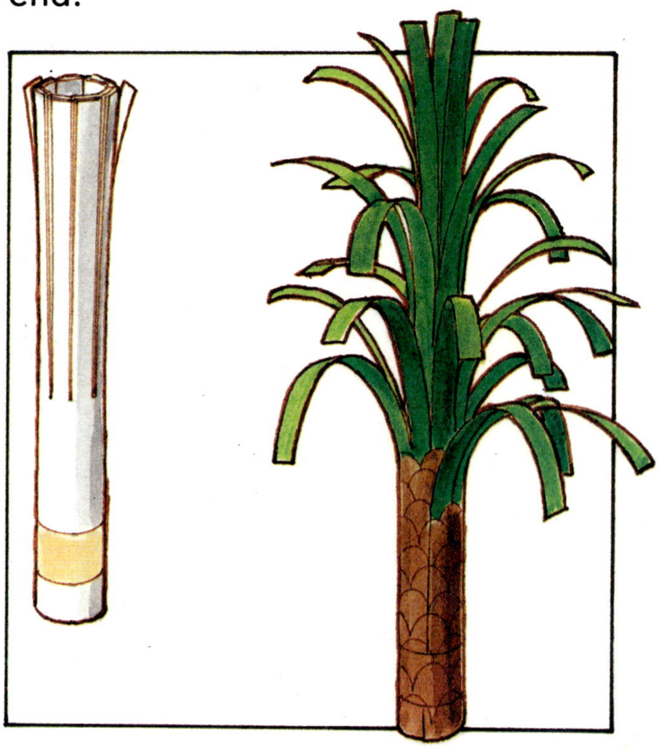

Hatch your own Dinosaur Eggs

What you need: balloons newspaper glue paste

1. Blow up the balloon and tie it up tightly with cotton.

2. Paste all over the balloon and then lay newspaper strips all over it. Paste all over the top of the newspaper and keep putting layers on top of the first one, until the egg is thick enough not to break.

3. Make sure it's smooth and covers the balloon completely. Now leave it to dry properly, then stick a pin through it carefully and pop the balloon inside.

4. You could paint the egg, or get someone to cut it open so that it looks like a hatched egg. Make little plasticine dinosaurs to hatch out of the egg.

MOSCHOPS STAYS AWAKE

It was evening in the land of the dinosaurs. The sun was going down. It was a bright orange ball on the horizon.

Ally and Moschops had been playing football all day. They sat down next to Flower, exhausted.

"Gosh, I'm tired," said Ally. He stretched and yawned. "I think I'll go to my cave and have a nice long sleep. Goodnight."

It was getting much darker, and the stars were beginning to come out. Moschops sat watching them twinkle. He didn't feel tired at all.

"Twinkle, twinkle, little star, how I wonder what you are." She closed up her petals to wait for the dawn.

"What can I do now?" Moschops said to himself. "I'm not at all sleepy. I want someone to play with."

Moschops went down to the lake. It was very dark, but he could see the moon reflected in the water. Mr. Ichthyosaurus was fast asleep.

Then he saw a shadowy shape. "Hello," he said, poking the shape. It didn't answer because it was a boulder!

Everything was very quiet. Moschops climbed to the top of a nearby hill. He could see lots of black shapes, and he could hear snoring.

"I suppose I ought to go to sleep," he thought. He lay down, but couldn't go to sleep. Then he had an idea . . .

He turned over and rolled all the way down the hill! It was great fun! He landed at the bottom with a bump.

He did it again. "Whoopee!" he shouted. And bumped into something very big. It was snoring.

It was Grandpa Diplodocus. "Oh no!" thought Moschops. If Grandpa woke up he would be very angry. But luckily he kept on snoring.

Moschops played all night, running up the hill, rolling down it, and dancing happily.

Then the sun rose slowly. Moschops could see the landscape stretched out before him. He rolled down the hill once more, and landed by Grandpa.

"Good morning," said Grandpa. "What a lovely day it's going to be!" "Yes," yawned Moschops. "I'm — yawn — going to sleep all the way through it." And he closed his eyes.